Quick Children's Speech Therapy At Home

Jane Bishop

Table of Contents

Introduction

There is probably nothing more typical of babyhood than baby speech. The child's first few words are among the greatest experiences of parenthood. They are written down in baby books, repeated to grandparents, neighbors, friends—anyone who will listen. They are a sign of growing up, the beginning of understanding between the child and his favorite adults. They are repeated proudly with all the childish errors of pronunciation and laughed over and enjoyed.

However, as the child matures, if his speech doesn't become as clear and easy to understand as that of other children of his age, the same parents and relatives who once imitated the baby talk and enjoyed it, begin to worry. They often criticize and attempt to correct the speech. In spite of this, many children enter school pronouncing some sounds incorrectly. . In school, the parents' criticisms, added to the teasing of classmates, help to make a child increasingly aware that he does not speak clearly. The classroom teacher attempts to help, but all too often, instead of actually knowing how to help the child, serves only to make him all the more aware of his inadequacy in expressing himself.

A public school speech correctionist can give the child the expert help he needs, but the classroom teacher, concerned with the progress of the group, has little time left in her crowded schedule to give concentrated individual aid. However, with the present dearth of trained speech specialists on school staffs, only a fraction of those children needing help can obtain it in the public schools. Thus the parents of the pre-school child with speech difficulties and the teachers of the kindergarten and first two grades are forced to become teachers of speech correction.

The material in this booklet has been brought together in the hope that both parents and teachers could find information and materials which might help children who do not produce common speech sounds clearly. It is hoped that it may prove useful to the many who cannot obtain the advice or services of a trained speech clinician.

These speech sound materials are the result of years of speech work with young children between the ages of four and eight, and with their mothers and fathers and classroom teachers. The overwhelming majority of very young children with unclear speech habits are those who have no major difficulties, either physical or emotional. Experience has shown that the parent or teacher, with a minimum of guidance from a specially trained speech correctionist, can do much to help these children speak well. The process of developing adult speech takes time and patience, and progress is found to be more rapid when a child is taught at home.

Many of the exercises may be found in speech correction text books. This is an attempt to simplify the standard procedures. Those exercises which might be misinterpreted or misused by parents or teachers who have no special training in speech correction have been eliminated. Whenever possible, however, the materials here presented should be used under supervision of an expert speech teacher to supplement the work.

Chapter One: The Story Of Jimmy

Jimmy was brought to a school speech clinic at five years of age. His mother and father had become worried about his speech, which seemed to them more childish than that of his neighborhood playmates. Strangers were hardly able to make out what Jimmy said. Only his best friends ignored it. Some children who had just moved into the neighborhood laughed at Jimmy and called him "baby." Jimmy had become increasingly shy of strange adults. He refused to go to the store on errands. He was afraid to go to the playground for fear of meeting the children who teased him.

When the speech teacher at school asked if the family had imitated and enjoyed baby talk it was learned that Jimmy's grandparents still were amused by his speech and were sure that he'd "just outgrow it." Jimmy's older brother Tom also had poor speech at first, but later he spoke perfectly at seven years. However, Tom's speech improved at a much earlier age. Jimmy heard his grandparents speak in their native language sometimes, but neither of his parents ever spoke it. He apparently had no understanding of any language which might have confused him in learning English.

His parents had begun to correct Jimmy. At first they just said the word which was mispronounced and asked him to repeat it. Usually Jimmy had been unable to correct himself. Then they had broken the word down into syllables, and found that Jimmy had difficulty with particular sounds within the word. He produced all syllables correctly except those which contained difficult sounds. Finally Jimmy had refused to repeat or to make any effort to correct his speech. Even when shamed about it in front of the other children, Jimmy had resented correction and stubbornly refused to attempt the difficult sounds. Naturally his mother and father did not want to see him singled out for unnecessary ridicule; neither did they want to spoil his usually pleasant personality, so they had asked the speech clinic teacher to advise them.

Before attempting any correction, the speech teacher had to consider many physical and other influencing factors which might determine a final decision to start speech training.

Jimmy's Growth Record

The first step in the teacher's check-up with Jimmy and his parents was a simple examination of the speech organs themselves. Jimmy was able to bring his tongue way out of his mouth and to point it. He then showed that he could wiggle it from side to side with agility. He could lift the tip and run it all over the upper lip and in the corners of his mouth like a cat licking milk from her whiskers. Since the muscles of his tongue were sufficiently controlled to do these exercises well, he proved that his tongue was capable of learning the rapid coordination necessary for good speech.

The second part of the examination showed that when Jimmy brought his jaws together, as if chewing gum, the lower teeth came inside the upper front teeth, and overlapped them partially. His jaws obviously made a good closure—the teeth were in good position for biting in front and for chewing in the sides. Like most five year olds, Jimmy had not yet begun to lose his baby teeth. In another year, the teacher explained, he might well be in the "ugly duckling" stage, with missing front teeth which might cause further speech difficulty.

The speech teacher then asked Jimmy's mother many questions about her son's general physical development. She found it had been normal. It was learned that Jimmy had been born at the end of a more or less full nine month pregnancy, during which his mother had not contracted a serious high fever illness or otherwise been seriously ill. He had exhibited no immediate difficulties after birth, eating and sleeping reasonably well. He was first nursed and then bottle fed.

Jimmy had been able to sit up without support by six months and had begun to walk at about thirteen months. By three years he was able to wash and toilet himself and to do many of the routine things in connection with dressing himself. He also was riding a three wheel bike and playing with other children under supervision from his mother. In short, his early development was as it should have been. However, Jimmy's mother admitted that he had been babied as the youngest child in a family often is. Although he was able to do many things for himself, he often asked and received help in doing things which his older brother had mastered somewhat earlier.

Jimmy's mother could not remember at first what children's diseases and high fever illnesses he had had in his early life. He seemed to have caught whatever the older brother brought home, but had had everything mildly and without sustained fever. He had had tonsilitis at two, with a running ear and earache. The family physician had removed this source of infection with an adenoid and tonsil operation and Jimmy had never had subsequent ear disturbances.

After learning of Jimmy's ear trouble, the speech teacher tested his hearing, in spite of the fact that he had carried out all verbal instructions and it was obvious that he heard. The teacher explained that sometimes children have a good deal of hearing in some pitches and still can't hear and learn speech accurately because of failure to hear at other pitches—especially true of children who mispronounce consonant sounds. It is possible that they do not have good hearing for the higher pitch levels in which these are made. Jimmy was able to hear and respond well to all of the tones on the hearing test, and the possibility that he spoke poorly because he heard poorly was eliminated.

When the teacher asked Jimmy's mother how old he had been when he first started talking, she said he had started babbling—syllables like "dada" and "mama"—at about six months. He had seemed to enjoy it when an adult babbled back at him. Then he had begun to imitate syllables, and by the time he was a year old he had three baby words in his vocabulary. "Dada" really meant "daddy" and "mama" was used only for his mother. He was also able to say "bye bye." By his second birthday he had been saying two and three word baby sentences: "Daddy bye bye"; "Me bye bye."

His speech development had been average and did not account for the delay in speech efficiency which disturbed his parents when he was five years old.

Finally the special speech teacher to whom they had brought Jimmy gave him a picture test containing all the English sounds. A collection of attractive pictures told a story and Jimmy named the objects and answered questions about them. He was able to pronounce the name of most of the objects and could understand the picture language. He had more or less average vocabulary for his age and an average understanding of language.

However, Jimmy's speech became hard to understand on certain parts of the test. He said "titty tat" for "kitty cat," "dun" for "gun." He knew what a "bath" was, but pronounced it "baff." He recognized "thumb" but pronounced it "fum." He also said "wed" for "red", "yike" for "like."

Mother And Dad Turn Teacher

When Jimmy was all through with the examination, the speech teacher told him that he had done very well indeed, and encouraged his mother and father by telling them that his speech difficulty probably could be overcome completely if they would give him some home lessons. Naturally, his parents were pleased and relieved to learn that he could be helped and that they could learn how to help their own son through his difficulties. Jimmy was already very aware of his "baby" pronunciation and they knew it would require individual encouragement and help at home before he started to school in the fall.

His mother was particularly pleased to know that there were ways to help him at home. She had already met the teacher in whose kindergarten class Jimmy would be enrolled. The teacher had said that many of her children would have trouble with some of the common speech sounds, but that aside from group speech games, she would be unable to help the individual child. A kindergarten crowded with children who have to learn to get used to and enjoy school, leaves little time for the teacher to help individuals within the group.

Chapter Two: How And Where Sounds Are Made

We have seen how the school's teacher of speech correction had to check into the physical, emotional and mental background of a child before determining how best he could be helped. The cause for poor speech had to be found before correction could be started. But before studying the causes of childish or poor speech in boys and girls it would be wise for us to discuss the way in which a child who speaks well makes the speech sounds and at what age a child can be expected to pronounce the speech sounds of the English language.

The consonant sounds in English may be described according to where they are made and how they are made. Some sounds are made by closing off the mouth and permitting the air stream to go out through the nose. These sounds, which are called nasal sounds, are M, N and NG. All other English sounds are made with the air sent through the mouth.

Most English sounds come in pairs, one whispered and one in which vibration can be felt in the throat. The sound SH as in "shoe" is whispered. Its teammate ZH like the SU in "treasure" is made in identically the same part of the mouth. However, SH is whispered; ZH is voiced. The difference can be appreciated by saying alternately SH and ZH with the hand upon the throat.

Perfect Speech Takes Time

The following letter groups indicate the sequence in which most children master consonant speech sounds.[*]

P, B, M, W, H.

T, D, N, G, K, NG, Y.

F.

V, TH (as in "then"), ZH, SH, L.

S, Z, R, WH, TH (as in "thin").

It should be noted that girls develop perfect speech on an average of one year before boys. In every neighborhood there are boys and girls who have virtually perfect speech by 4.5 years. It is possible, with adequate and interesting speech play at home, for many children who are mentally, physically and emotionally strong, to have near-perfect pronunciation by the time they enter kindergarten.

---

[*] Parents should keep in mind that certain sounds such as M, N and W rarely present problems in normal speech development. For this reason these sounds have been omitted from the list for which example lessons are given at the end of this booklet.

Chapter Three: Causes Of Faulty Speech

The mechanics of making sounds and the speech development of a youngster are basic to discovering the cause of difficulties. With a thorough knowledge of the growth and history of a child, a speech correctionist can determine the particular needs of a boy or girl. Some of the causes of poor speech in a child are:

Extremely poor bite. Some children have lower jaws receding or jutting forward so greatly that the lower front teeth never meet the upper front teeth in biting. This may make it difficult to produce sounds, especially F, V and TH. A normal bite requires that the front teeth meet with the lowers, sliding behind the uppers until part of the lower teeth are hidden from view.

Tongue-tie. If a child can bring the tip of his tongue in front of the teeth and lift it sufficiently to say T or D clearly, he is not tongue-tied as far as speech is concerned. In the present day, when most children are hospital-born, rarely is a child's tongue so tightly attached to the floor of the mouth as to influence his speech.

Faulty development of teeth. Extremely poor spacing or missing teeth sometimes makes sound production difficult. Especially hard to produce are the TH and perhaps S and Z sounds. If upper teeth are missing in front, F and V are difficult. Since missing teeth in childhood are a part of normal dentition, speech work is sometimes postponed until these teeth appear. Bands and braces may cause the child to adjust his usual tongue movements to them. When the dentist removes them, the child will once more have to adjust his speech to this change within his mouth.

Mouth breathing. Some children, either because of a broken nose or other obstruction, such as adenoids, cannot produce M, N or NG sounds. They sound as if they had a cold and are likely to breathe through the open mouth. Chronic mouth-breathing not connected with a common cold always should be checked by a physician for nasal obstructions.

Slow specific development. Average speech development would require the child to use and associate several words with actual things by the time he was a year old. At two he should be able to use baby sentences of two or three words. Girls usually develop a greater vocabulary and clearer speech sooner than boys. If a child does not begin to use sentences until three years or later, it is possible that his whole speech development is behind schedule. It follows that such a child would be very unlikely to have mastered all the speech sounds before school age.

Poor coordination. If a child shows late development of general coordination, it is possible that his speech muscles also are delayed in developing the very fine coordination necessary for good speech. If he has difficulty in deciding which hand to favor in feeding, grasping a pencil, etc., this too may have influenced his finer muscular coordinations. It is usual for a six-months old baby to sit up unsupported. At one year the average child walks and at three he can usually dress and feed himself and ride a three wheel bike.

General health. Children who have been continually ill during the early years of life often are late in speaking. There is little need to develop speech when one is sick or bedridden. General chronic illness may account for slow development of skill in articulation.

Hearing lost. Untreated ear infections or high fever illnesses may leave a child with permanent hearing losses. Some children are born with imperfect hearing. The partially hard of hearing child may first call attention to this defect by developing defective speech. When a child has defective speech the family doctor might be asked to check the ears and, if necessary, to refer the child to an ear specialist.

Home Influences On Speech

A child's speech development may be seriously influenced not only by physical handicaps but also by the people closest to him. The youngest child in a family usually hears patterns of clearer speech from his older brothers and sisters. However, if the oldest has poor speech, the younger children are likely to imitate his defective sounds, even though the parents provide a standard of good speech. Where there is a foreign language spoken at home, the child often has the problem of learning the sounds in two languages at the same time.

Children will imitate the speech standards in the neighborhood as well as the home. If all the other children have poor speech there is little incentive to improve and no good model to follow among the playmates.

Some sincere but ill-advised attempts at correction in the home can actually hold back a child's development. Such efforts include:

Comparison with other children. Parents too often make the mistake of comparing a child unfavorably with a younger or older sister or brother or with neighborhood children. A child who feels reason to doubt his family's love and need for him will resent especially the comparison. By comparing unfavorably his speech with that of others, parents cause the child to lose fundamental confidence in himself and to resent any attention whatever being called to his speech.

No need for good speech. A child may not choose to grow up if it seems more profitable to remain a baby. Sometimes a child is given little chance to grow up. If he is greatly babied he has little need to grow in speech habits either.

Desire for perfection. Parents who are forever stopping the child in the midst of the things he is trying to say in order to correct his pronunciation are likely to cause him to be negative and sullen to all criticism. This is especially true if the child is criticized in front of other children. Of course parents want their children to be perfect, but too much insistence on perfection will never help the child to achieve good speech.

Faulty Speech For No Apparent Reason

A word of caution—remember that all children develop at their individual rates in speech as in everything else. Many children show no obvious physical or emotional problem serious enough to be called the cause of faulty speech. These are apparently normal, healthy and happy children who happen never to have corrected their infantile speech. They should respond easily and eagerly to speech work and can be helped a great deal by their parents. Fortunately, the vast majority of very young children with unclear speech habits fall into this group. It is to help these children and their parents that the following example lessons, materials and games have been compiled.

Chapter Four: Helping Your Child With His Speech

When a mother checks for trouble spots she perhaps can tell from the child's everyday speech just what sounds he cannot say correctly. Just to be sure she is right she gives him the articulation test found in this ebook. After reading the directions on the score page carefully, she becomes familiar with the form on which she is to check sounds he finds troublesome. She notes what words are to be used, what sounds within the words she is to listen for. Most sounds appear in three positions illustrated by three different words—in the first of these words the sound being checked will be at the beginning, in the second word, the middle, and in the third, at the end of the word. She compares the score sheet with the picture sheets and sees that each picture has a key word matching it on the score sheet. Perhaps the child's father could keep score in another part of the room while his mother has him say the words.

The mother shows the pictures to her child and prompts him to say the word which is illustrated. When he has trouble identifying the picture, she helps him by saying, "What is this?" When the name of the object is unfamiliar, the mother says the word for him first and has him repeat it. If he mispronounces the underlined sound, she puts a check beside the same word on the score sheet. She is only concerned with the sound underlined.

A Game Not A Test

The pictures from the articulation test are presented as a game rather than a test, which would be dull for the child who may resent corrections. The mother is careful not to make the test drudgery because it is the first taste her child has had of speech work. If he finds it unpleasant, he will not want to do any more.

To make the game more interesting and not repetitive go to http://images.google.com and search for words-pictures listed on pages 29-31.

You can show the pictures on the screen or preferably print them out. He cuts out the pictures and, with the help of his father, pastes them on individual cardboards approximately penny postal size. His picture cards are now ready for future speech games.

When the mother has completed the picture or articulation test, she takes the score sheet and on a separate piece of paper lists all the sounds —not words—that the child has difficulty in saying. This makes it very clear just exactly what sounds are to be learned. In this child's case the mother has written on her list that she must teach him to say R, L, TH, F, V, S, Z and CH.

Silent Mirror Games

Before the mother decides what sound to teach first, she begins the lesson by having the youngster practice lip and tongue games in front of the mirror. This accustoms him to the idea of working in front of a mirror and to the lip and tongue movements he will need in learning the sounds. Here are some of the games both the mother and child play together.

1. Bring the lips together and separate them quickly, saying ba-ba-ba-ba like a lamb, ma-ma-ma-ma like a baby and peep-peep-peep-peep like a baby bird.

2. Round the lips for oo, then retract or pull them back quickly for ee. It sounds like a fireman's siren.

When the child can move his lips rapidly, they try some tongue exercises.

1. Stick out the tongue like a cat, point it, and quickly lick all around the lips.

2. Next put the tongue tip up behind the upper teeth (careful to touch the ridge behind the teeth, not the teeth). Quickly flick the tongue down behind the lower teeth. It may help to pretend to be whisper ing la-la-la-la.

3. Be careful to keep the tip of the tongue down behind the lower front teeth. At the same time, raise the back part of the tongue up to touch the roof of the mouth, next lower the back of the tongue quickly. Repeat the movement of the back part of the tongue rapidly withou ever moving the tongue tip from behind the lower front teeth. The back of the tongue jumps up! Jumps down!

After practicing these games in front of the mirror, the mother takes the mirror away in order to see if her son can make these motions without looking. When he can, he is ready to begin work with the sounds themselves.

Choosing The First Sound

The mother has in front of her the list of sounds her child cannot say correctly. Wisely, she decides to start with an easy sound, one that can be learned quickly. She reasons that if her child can master one sound rapidly, he will be eager to learn more and will think his new "game" is fun. She decides to begin with V and F.

This proves to be a good choice. Both of these sounds are made with the lips and teeth and are easily seen and easily learned. When the mother has run through the list to try out the sounds for difficulty, she decides on the V and F sounds because her child imitates these easily.

Word Repetition

In her first lesson she tries to have the child repeat a simple word like "four" after her. Like many children he cannot repeat the word accurately after his mother said it. She thought that if he could imitate her easily, he would have a good chance of learning his new sounds rapidly. But, unfortunately, few children are able to learn new sounds merely by repeating. If they could it would be unlikely that they would have learned speech incorrectly in the first place. It takes more than simple repetition of words to teach new sounds; they must be seen and felt.

Mirror Play

After trying the repetition method for a very few minutes, the mother sits down with her child in front of a mirror. The mirror serves to help the child get his lips and teeth in the correct position for the new sound. First he looks in the mirror to see how his mother places her lips; then he looks at himself and tries to get his in the same position. As they both watch, the mother says "Four." With his lower lip tucked under his upper teeth, as it should be for F, he says, "Four" too. He is able to say the word correctly at the first try. If he were not able to keep his lip where it should have been, his mother might have helped him by lightly holding it in position. After she has done this once, he will try again to do it himself. Now, still watching the mirror, he says, "Four" several times. He continues to do it correctly. Now, with his back to the mirror, he tries again. He isn't quite as sure of his speech movements this time and "four" does not sound as distinct as before. After saying the word again with the aid of the mirror, he turns away and this time is successful. He practices saying "Four" a few more times without looking. He says it correctly each time. It means that he not only knows how F looks, but how it feels.

Word Games

At the first lesson the child does not attempt more than five words. His mother realizes that he is just a youngster and cannot be expected immediately to sit down and learn the long word lists. After learning "Four" he tries other simple words beginning with F. His mother is careful to select words from his own vocabulary. Instead of monotonously going over and over the words, she makes a game out of them. She presents the delighted child with a new scrapbook. All of its pages are empty. Before the lesson started she cut pictures representing these words out of magazines. When she gives him the book, she tells him that if he can say the new words correctly, he may paste their pictures in his new book. He does very well. Of the five words he has tried to learn this first day, he is able to say three correctly without looking in the mirror and without help from his mother. These three pictures are pasted in the scrapbook. The other two words are saved for the next lesson.

Success in Brevity

The first speech lesson is over. It has been fun and the child is eager to have another lesson in order that he may paste those other two pictures in the scrapbook. During the day he turns to the scrapbook with pleasure and talks about the time when it will be full of pictures. The reason he is so pleased with his speech work is because his wise mother works with him only a few minutes. She is not overly critical and instead of saying, "That's wrong, do it right," she mildly but firmly suggests that he try again. When he has said a word correctly, she shows that she is genuinely pleased; when he has said it incorrectly, she shows him how to do it right with no criticism. She remembers that she is working with a child. He cannot keep doing the same thing too long. He needs the same word presented in several ways to keep up his interest. He needs praise and a feeling of success.

Since he is young, it is not possible for his mother to keep his attention more than ten minutes with various activities. However, a still younger child may be unable to work for more than a few minutes. It is always best to attempt speech play at a time when the household is quiet and when both the child and the mother are rested and calm. A great amount of excitement prevents much accomplishment in the way of corrective speech. Both calm attitude and surroundings are a requisite whenever a mother or father and child try constructive speech work together.

Listening Carefully

The mother continues with her daily ten minute speech periods for the next few lessons. She reviews the words beginning with F and progresses to words ending in F. Later she tries those in which F appears in the middle. Though she keeps mirror close at hand, she does not have to use it as frequently as she once did since her child has become accustomed to making the F sound according to the feel of it. As well as becoming aware of seeing and feeling F, he is learning something else. He begins to appreciate when a word with F in it is said incorrectly. The mother has been a great help in encouraging the child to listen more carefully to what is said. Both of them will enjoy the listening game.

In this game the mother recites a list of words she and her youngster have used previously. Some of the words she says correctly, some she says incorrectly. Whenever she makes a mistake the child claps his hands. They keep score in the back of the scrapbook and on the days when his score is 0 the youngster is pleased to see that he didn't miss hearing one of the "wrong" words. Listening carefully is very important in learning to talk correctly. When listening carefully to adults, the child learns new words correctly. When his mother hears him correct himself, as he talks to her in everyday conversation, she knows that he hears himself make mistakes and is pleased that he can now correct himself. This is a real step forward.

When To Start A New Sound

The mother rightly feels that this self-correction is the best indication that it is time for another sound. She realizes that she should not wait for the child to say all of his F words correctly every time. She is satisfied that a few are established in everyday speech and that there are indications, through his self-correction, that there soon will be others. Even with less success, she will feel that it is better to leave one sound and go on to another rather than risk losing his interest through monotony and an implication of failure. If he ever comes to feel that speech work is drudgery, he will become stubborn and refuse to cooperate. However, he is doing well and it is time to learn V sounds.

Voiced And Whispered Sounds

The child learns to pronounce V in the same way as he learned F. His mother shows him that it is made in the same manner, that is, by lightly biting the lower lip. Again she starts with simple words beginning with V, then teaches words where the V is on the end and in the middle. By this time the mirror work is not as important as learning to feel and hear the sound. Although F and V are made, with the lip in the same position, they feel and sound different. The mother shows this to him by having her child place his finger on his lower lip and say "fairy" and then "very", prolonging the first sounds. When he says "fairy" he feels just air and no vibration on his finger as when he said F. When he says "very", his lip vibrates and there is not much air coming out. If he placed his fingers on his throat instead of on his lip, he could feel the same difference in vibration between F and V. But he does not confuse the sounds, so his mother does not stress this point. However, as they work on more difficult sounds later, the distinction of feel and sound in the case of the two made in the same position becomes very important.

Using New Sounds In Play

The mother's success with her home speech correction program results from her patient understanding and her ability to plan interesting lessons. She knows that a small child cannot sit down as in school and respond to formal lessons. This is the wiggly age. To hold his attention, sounds of other play activities going on in the house have to be eliminated. Eventually the short periods of speech work are established as a matter of routine. It is an enjoyable routine because the games are fun. The child also feels that he is making progress. There are more pictures in his scrap-book. He is proud of his mother's obvious approval of his cooperation.

The mother is careful not to expect too much. She knows that she and the child cannot have the same appreciation of good speech. She also knows that he should never be made to feel upset about his mispronunciations, so she does not stress perfect speech. She is very careful not to over-correct in practice, and corrects only those sounds learned previously. For instance, in the word "fairy" she lets him say "faiwy" until they have both worked on the R sound. And as she hears him talking about the house she doesn't correct every mispronounced word. She remembers he can be resentful of too much correction. There are many words which her youngster does well in practice but does not carry over into everyday usage. She realizes that further review in terms of games and an increased awareness of correct speech will bring results in due time. Patience and ingenuity are the keys to her success.

Fitting The Program

Of course, not all children are alike. Some may resent the play aspect and prefer to sit down to formal drill and practice. By all means, the child should have his word list, sentence and story drill. On the other hand there are children too young in behavior to do anything but the smallest amount of practice and games.

These children have to be drawn into this new activity gradually. Great care is necessary to avoid antagonism through the child's lack of understanding of what is expected. The basis of successful home speech improvement is found in a real understanding of the child and his specific speech problem, then putting him to work accordingly. The following check-list for correction serves as a brief sketch of the first home lesson.

The Home Correction Program in Brief

1. Give the child the articulation or picture test, carefully noting just exactly what sounds are made incorrectly.

2. Test the movements of his lips and tongue to determine whether they can move accurately and swiftly for speech.

3. Spend some time on the lip and tongue exercises found on page 18.

4. See what sound you are going to teach first by seeing which one the child imitates most readily.

5. If the child can repeat correctly the sound you have said, begin to put this sound in the beginning of simple one-syllable words, next on the ends of words, and finally in the middle of words.

6. However, if he cannot easily repeat the sound after you, use a mirror to show him how to place his lips and tongue. Consult the charts at the beginning of each exercise sheet for accurate placement.

7. After a few tries at making the sound by itself in front of the mirror, the child should make it in the beginning of words. Be sure that his lips and tongue are in the right position.

8. Turn him away from the mirror to test whether or not he can pronounce these words correctly without the help of the mirror.

9. Play a listening game to detect whether or not he can tell by ear when the sound is pronounced correctly and when it is incorrect.

10. When the sound is being consistently learned in its beginning position in the word, go ahead and teach it in the end and middle of words.

11. Proceed to a new sound as soon as the child is beginning to use a few corrected words in his conversation.

12. Consult word lists, poems and games on the following pages as suggestions for practice materials for individual sounds.

Chapter Five: The Articulation Test

Directions for scoring: As you show the pictures to your child, let him name the word in each picture.

If he does not know the word, or gives another word, ask him to repeat the correct word after you. Mark with an X the box opposite each word corresponding to the picture. Do not mark it as wrong if the PARTICULAR SOUND which you are testing within the word is correctly produced. For example, if he has the first P but the final L incorrect in the first word, pencil, do not mark the word as incorrect. Double consonants, as in the word "rabbit" are pronounced only once. If he omits the tested sound entirely, mark it as incorrect.

Pencil

Apple

Cup

Boat

Rabbit

Tub

Mouse

Hammer

Drum

Wheel

Wagon

Sandwich

Fork

Telephone

Knife

Valentine

Stove

Thimble

Birthday

Bath

Feather

Top

Letter

Cat

Dog

Indian

Bed

Nail

Banana

Clown

Soap

Policeman

Bus

Zebra

Scissors

Dolls

Lamp

Ba<u>ll</u>oon

Be<u>ll</u>

<u>R</u>ope

A<u>rr</u>ow

Bea<u>r</u>

<u>Sh</u>oe

Bru<u>sh</u>es

Fi<u>sh</u>

Gara<u>ge</u>

<u>Church</u>

Mat<u>ch</u>es

<u>J</u>ack in the Box

En<u>g</u>ine

Bri<u>dg</u>e

<u>C</u>ar

Ba<u>sk</u>et

Boo<u>k</u>

<u>G</u>un

Wa<u>g</u>on

Fla<u>g</u>

Mo<u>nk</u>ey (ng)

Swi<u>ng</u>

<u>Y</u>es

Chapter Six: P And B Sounds

P and B are made by putting the lips together lightly and then separating them quickly with a slight explosion of air.

P is said without any vibration in the throat.

B is made with the voice.

P And B Words

pie	cup	paper	be	tub	rubber
pail	top	puppy	boy	rub	baseball
pick	up	supper	bed	bib	baby
pat	lip	happy	big	scrub	number
penny	nap	sleepy	bath	knob	good-bye
pig	cap	helping	ball	sob	about
pin	lap	Skippy	book	cub	rubbing
pants	keep	apple	bowl	grab	robin

pull	peep	pumpkin	boat	crib	Bobby
pop	stop	zipper	back	fib	nobody

P And B Story

Bobby gets up from his nap to go out to play. Before he goes out he gets all dressed up in his pants, shirt, coat, and cap. He eats an apple as he goes. He plays baseball in the back yard. Soon it is time to come in again. He says good-bye to his playmates and goes inside to have supper. First he gets out of his clothes by pulling the zipper down and then he takes a bath in the wash bowl. He has a cup of soup for supper, a potato, some pudding and an apple. After supper he sits in mother's lap while she reads him a story out of a book. It is a story about a puppy and a robin. Then he goes to bed.

(You can tell your child this story in parts and ask him to repeat it, or you can tell it with magazine pictures and he can help by filling in details. The object is to have him say a word in the drill without your telling it to him first.)

P And B Rhymes

Put the baby's supper on the table
Put the puppy's toy bone on the floor
Put the pies at everybody's place

And we'll all say please when we want more.

Chapter Seven: F And V Sounds

F and V are made by gently biting the lower lip, keeping the upper lip out of the way.
F is said without any vibration in the throat.
V is made with a definite vibration.

F And V Words

for	safe	elephant	valley	love	overalls
far	laugh	telephone	visit	drive	seven
fire	enough	coffee	violin	wave	river
funny	roof	laughing	vine	five	cover
find	leaf	office	vest	above	every
feel	cough	coughing	value	behave	never
foot	calf	before	village	have	heavy
food	shelf	offer	vegetable	move	even

farm	off	sofa	vacuum	give	having
face	half	muffin	vase	live	giving

F And V Story

A house is burning. Who is going to put out the fire? The fireman learned about the fire on the telephone. Because the fireman got some smoke in his throat he is coughing.

(Be sure to phrase your questions in such a way that the child is able to supply you with the word you want to practice.)

F And V Rhyme

This is a very funny man
Who laughs and laughs all day
With funny face and great big feet
We'd love to have him stay.
And we'll all say please when we want more.

Chapter Eight: TH Sound

There are two TH sounds. Both are made by sticking the tongue out of the mouth slightly, and blowing air out over the tongue.

The first TH is made without any voice or vibration in the throat. For the second TH be sure there is vibration in the throat.

TH Words

thank	mouth	nothing	this	bathe	father
three	teeth	birthday	that	with	neither
thirsty	tooth	something	the	teethe	brother
thumb	bath	anything	those	smooth	other
thunder	both	toothbrush	them	scythe	either
thimble	truth	something	their		feather

think	fourth	plaything	these		bathing
thick	path	bath tub	though		weather
thin	cloth	bath towel	then		gather
throw	moth	Arthur			

TH Story

This is Ruth's birthday. She is three years old. She has a birthday cake with candles. There are presents from mother, father and brother. She opens her presents. Mother gave her a thimble. Father gave her a ball to throw. Brother gave her a toothbrush. Everybody gave her something for her birthday. Then she put their presents away and they all sat down to eat the birthday cake.

(With the help of some pictures elaborate the story of Ruth's birthday party. All that is needed is a picture of a little girl, a birthday cake and some other pictures representing presents.)

TH Rhyme

This is the boat the family built
That mother and father and brother built

This is the boat the family built

That's really for brother and me.

Chapter Nine: T And D Sounds

T and D are made by placing the tip of the tongue up behind the upper teeth ridge, not touching the teeth. The tongue is then brought down quickly as the sound is made with a little explosion of air.

T is made with no throat vibration. D is made with definite vibrations in the throat.

T And D Words

top	cat	butter	dog	bird	today
table	coat	city	dish	sled	lady
time	kite	sister	doll	bead	under
tire	salt	sometime	doctor	bad	candy
tongue	soft	party	day	head	somebody
toe	boat	bottom	dirty	mud	muddy
telephone	nest	better	deep	cold	Indian
tea	tent	potato	dime	told	window

44

tap	nut	pity	do	played	ready
tip	put	letter	duck	bed	daddy

T And D Story

This is the story of Teddy. Teddy is a dog. Teddy, the dog, just woke up. He got up from his master's bed and went to the window. Then he ran down stairs to his breakfast. He found a potato and some butter but he did not eat them. Teddy jumped on to the table and knocked the telephone down. Somebody then put Teddy out of doors. Teddy dug in the ground, played with a duck, tried to catch a kite, and he got al muddy. He even played with daddy's tire. He got so dirty his master took him inside and gave him a bath in a tub. Last of all Teddy went to sleep under the bed.

(Be sure to have a toy dog or pictures of a dog.)

T And D Rhyme

Dottie had a little dog
And Tommy had a cat.
Dottie made the dog a dress
And the kitty wore a hat.

Chapter Eleven: S And Z Sounds

 S and Z are made by forcing air out of the mouth over the lifted tip of the tongue, which is almost touching the ridge behind the upper gum. The teeth are brought almost together. S is made without any vibration in the throat. Z is made with throat vibration.

S And Z Words

see	face	pencil	zoo	size	visit
say	guess	saucer	zebra	fuzz	easy
saw	this	fussy	zone	tease	busy
same	circus	bicycle	zipper	as	daisy
soap	looks	grocer	zip	does	buzzing
city	laughs	myself	zig-zag	has	Wednesday
sun	bus	answer		his	music

sand	cups	useful		scissors	present
store	hats	seesaw		these	lazy
soup	house	inside		those	visitor

S And Z Story

We are going to a store on Wednesday. To get to the store we will ride in a bus. We will buy cups, soap, soup and maybe a see-saw. See the scissors, and there is a zipper. What would you like to buy? Do you like the bicycle? Here is a toy zebra in a toy zoo. Now it is time to go back to our house.

(These words might lend themselves to a story about shopping. Have a picture of a store which is filled with objects; then compose the story around this picture.)

S And Z Rhyme

The zebra lives in the zoo
The rattlesnake lives there too
The snake slides and hisses
And the zebra just misses
When he tries to slide and hiss too.

Chapter Eleven: SH And ZH Sounds

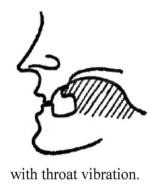 Bring the teeth almost together. Place the tongue tip up near the ridge as for S and slide it somewhat forward, so that the part just behind the tip is now near the ridge. Round the lips and protrude them slightly. SH is made without throat vibration as if whispering. ZH is made with throat vibration.

SH And ZH Words

shoe	push	pushing		garage	measure
sheep	dish	brushes		rouge	decision
show	smash	sunshine		massage	pleasure
shut	fish	fishing		corsage	occasion
shake	brush	ocean			division
she	crash	nation			explosion
shout	bush	crushes			treasure

ship	splash	dishes			
shirt	fresh	finishing			
should	wash	washing			

SH And ZH Story

This is a story of a little girl who helps her mother. This little girl puts her shoes away, hangs up her shirt and then closes the closet door. Now mother shows her how to brush the crumbs from the table as well as how to carry the dishes into the kitchen and wash them.

(Words like shoe, shirt, dish and wash could be practiced in your every day situations.)

SH And ZH Rhyme

Fishing a big fish out of the ocean

Shaking its tail splashing the ship

Measure him carefully and throw him back in again

Splash and he's off again under the ship.

Chapter Eleven: CH And J Sounds

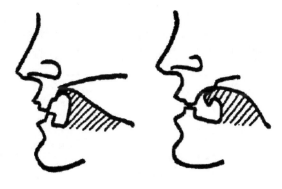

CH and J are actually combinations of sounds previously studied. CH is made by saying T and SH and gradually making the two more and more closely combined. CH is said without throat vibration.

J is a combination of D and ZH. The two sounds are said in a rapid blending. J is made with throat vibration.

CH And J Words

child	watch	matches	jump	cage	engine
chair	teach	teacher	Jack	page	orangeade
chin	touch	richer	Jill	bridge	angel
cheese	march	butcher	giant	edge	pages
chop	catch	churches	jacket	change	dangerous

cheek	match	catching	jelly	large	enjoy
chocolate	reach	touching	joke	strange	vegetable
chase	much	pitcher	just	garbate	largest
chose	pitch	kitchen	jaw	package	magic
children		watching	jar	orange	suggest

CH And J Story

The child sits in a chair watching mother make chocolate cookies. The mother puts the jelly in a jar, the left over vegetables go in the garbage, and a pitcher of orangeade into the ice box. Then she puts the matches away where children's fingers cannot reach them. After the kitchen is all clean, they go into the dining room to eat some cheese.

(These words might be worked into kitchen activities. In your own kitchen, or a fictional one in a picture, develop situations requiring the use of these words.)

CH And J Rhyme

Cookies in the kitchen

Jam in the jar

Children's fingers reaching

But they're just too far.

Chapter Twelve: R And ER Sounds

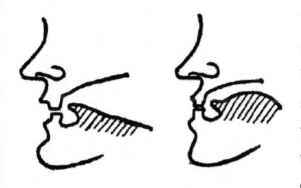 When R is the first sound in a word or is followed by a vowel it has a sound somewhat different from the R sound as made as the last sound in a word or when followed by a consonant. Note the difference in pronouncing R in "run", "red" and in "father", "mother."

In both sounds the lips should not be too greatly rounded lest the child say W instead. The sound is made by flapping the tip of the tongue up toward, but never touching, the roof of the mouth.

The ER is made in the same manner as R but with a very tense back of the tongue. Both are made with throat vibration.

R And ER Words

ring	very			father	bird
run	around			mother	hurt

red	carry			brother	pearl
wrap	story			chair	thirty
rope	carrot			collar	forty
rug	orange			door	thirsty
rose	sorry			car	learn
rain	garden			hard	first
rabbit	parrot			four	third
river	arrow				surely

R And ER Story

Father, mother, and brother all went for a walk in the woods. In the woods they saw a rabbit who was hopping around, a bird who had hurt his leg, and a garden of roses. They saw a thirsty chipmunk drinking from the river. All of a sudden it began to rain very hard and they had to run home.

(This story could be drawn as you tell it, or you could illustrate with magazine pictures. Have the child retell all of these stories to you to make sure he can say the words correctly.)

R And ER Rhyme

The Parrot and the Scarecrow

Met by the large haystack

The Scarecrow roared at the Parrot

But the bird just answered him back.

Chapter Thirteen: L And EL Sounds

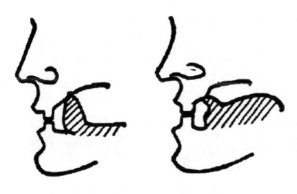

There is a slight difference between the L sound in "live", "love" and that in "bell", "felt." However, both are made by raising the tip of the tongue and flapping it up against the ridge behind the upper gums.

The EL sound as it is used at the end of a word or when followed by a consonant is made in exactly the same way but by tensing the back part of the tongue a little more. Both L sounds are made with throat vibrations.

L And EL Words

lady	follow			belt	bell
late	balloon			felt	doll

like	belong			fault	wall
lion	alone			colt	ball
lose	silly			shelf	pail
left	dolly			sails	small
lamp	pillow			sells	tall
laugh	telephone			shawl	fell
living	elephant			salt	tell
lie	jelly			smelt	call

L And EL Story

The doll is to be the lady of the house. The doll has a living room. There is a picture on the wall and she has a pillow on the sofa. Dolly also has a telephone. She likes to lie down on her sofa in the living room and talk on the telephone. When it gets dark she turns on a light. Now it is time for dolly to go to bed.

(Play house with the child. This situation might be played out with actual toys and the words practiced as the toys are handled.)

L And EL Rhyme

The silly elephant worked all day
While the lion slept in his stall
The elephant laughed at the lazy beast
Who dreamed he had done it all.

Chapter Fourteen: K And G Sounds

The K and G sounds are made by opening the mouth and raising the back of the tongue until it touches the back part of the roof of the mouth. The tongue is then dropped from this position with an explosion of sound.

K is made without throat vibration. The G sound is made with throat vibration.

K And G Words

cup	take	monkey	gun	wagon	big
candy	talk	cookie	go	biggest	dog
cow	walk	basket	get	forget	bag
king	stick	circus	goose	tiger	hug
curtain	drink	because	gas	sugar	pig
car	thank	pumpkin	give	begin	leg

cold	ask	buckle	garden	organ	rug
count	milk	walking	game	together	dig
coat	book	pocket	good	angry	flag
cap	duck	jacket	gone	again	frog

K And G Story

(Instead of the usual story, have an imaginary telephone conversation with the child. Let him call you up on a toy phone and then you can steer the conversation into the use of the words above. Maneuver the conversation in such a way that he says the word without first hearing it from you. For example, ask him what he wears if he goes out on a cold day, what does he drink for breakfast, what animal says bow-wow, and so forth. If he says an expected word incorrectly, hang up; practice the word for a while and then let him call you again.)

K And G Rhyme

Monkey's in the circus
Climbing up a stick
Joking with a tiger
Who's feeling kind of slick.

Chapter Fifteen: Games

Every child likes to play games. There is no reason why his speech work cannot be done in play form. For this purpose there are listed below some games which you may adapt to the teaching of all or certain sounds. This teaching through play will help you to encourage the usage of new sounds in everyday speech. This method will help bridge the gap between making the sound correctly in daily practice and the more difficult business of making it a part of his conversation. These games are only suggestions. Your own imagination for new materials will be a wonderful help. Here are some suggestions to get you started.

Fishing Game

 Have pictures representing words which contain the sounds you have been working on. Put paper clips on each picture; then put these pictures in a toy pail or box. Attach a magnet to a string hanging from a pole. To play the game your child will fish for the pictures in the pail by trying to have the magnet catch on to the paper clip. After lifting the picture out of the pail, the child tries to say the name of the picture correctly. If he does, he may keep the picture; if he does not, he must put the picture back (after having practiced it a little) and try again.

Matching Game

Have two identical sets of cards. Lay down one set face up on the table. Hold the other set in your hand face down and ask the child to choose a card. He takes the card, looks at it, and then tries to say its name correctly. If he does, he looks around to find which card on the table it matches. After he finds its partner he puts his card on top of the one on the table. If he has not said the name of the card correctly, it is set aside for practice.

Spinning Game

You can make a cardboard spinner by taking a large piece of card-board and fastening a movable arrow to the center by using a screw. The arrow must be able to spin around. Place pictures around the cardboard in a circle. Then let the child spin the arrow. When the arrow stops at a picture, have the child name the picture. If he says the name correctly, put the picture in one pile; if he says it incorrectly, start another pile. Of course the object is to have just one pile of correctly pronounced names.

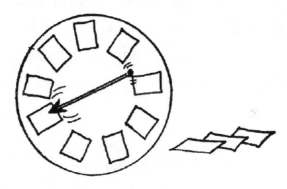

Box Game

Place two attractive boxes side by side. Again have a set of pictures representing learned words. Present these pictures to the child and as he says the sound correctly place the picture in one box; if he should make a mistake, put that card in the other box. After finishing the card once, take out those that were mispronounced and this time try by saying the words correctly to put them in the other box.

Hide-and-Seek Game

Hide objects or pictures representing words being practiced about the room. After the child finds the object or picture have him try to say the word correctly. There will be two piles, a correct one and an incorrect one. Practice the incorrect pile, then hide the objects and pictures again to see if the next time he can say them right.

Nonsense Tree

This is a make-believe tree that grows as the child is able to say his practice words correctly. First simply draw the trunk of a tree, then as the child is able to say his words right, add branches upon which hang tiny pictures of the objects which he can name.

Freight Train Game

On a sheet of paper draw an engine, then have the child try to pronounce correctly the names he has been practicing. As he is able to say the names of objects correctly, draw a box car and include a picture of the object he could name. Keep practicing your other drill words until they too can be included in the train.

A Pretend Party

This is an extension of the articulation test. Wrap up pictures or tiny objects whose names you have been practicing into attractive party packages. After the child has opened the package and extracted the picture or object, he tries to say its name correctly. If he does, he can keep the object or picture; if he can't, he will practice and try it during the next lesson period.

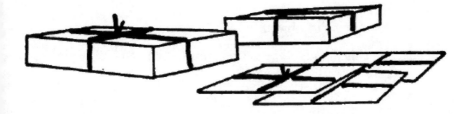

Speech Tea Party

This game is suggested to help you have a practice period for words other than nouns or names of things. At this tea party tell the child he is going to practice saying words like "is", "was, "going", "have" and many others correctly. During the party give the child an opportunity to say these words; if he says them wrong, note it for future drill.

House That Jack Built

Keep a scrapbook dedicated to the building of a house. On the cover of the book, have a picture of the house. On the first page you might have a picture of the family living there. Furnish the house with objects which the child is able to pronounce correctly. Have the family do common things, such as having a picnic, so that your child may have some practice using connecting words that are not just the names of things.

Made in the USA
Lexington, KY
24 May 2015